UNITED STATES
the land

Marlene Greil

A Bobbie Kalman Book

The Lands, Peoples, and Cultures Series

Crabtree Publishing Company

www.crabtreebooks.com

The Lands, Peoples, and Cultures Series
Created by Bobbie Kalman

Author: Marlene Greil

Editor: Lynn Peppas

Proofreader: Rachel Eagen

Photo research: Crystal Sikkens, Planman Technologies

Editorial director: Kathy Middleton

Design: Planman Technologies

Production coordinator: Margaret Amy Salter

Prepress technician: Margaret Amy Salter

Print coordinator: Katherine Berti

Written, developed, and produced by Planman Technologies

Cover: Photographer overlooking Grand Canyon

Title page: The twin peaks of the Maroon Bells and Maroon Lake in the White River National Forest of Colorado

Back cover: Bald Eagle

Icon: Bison

Illustrations:
Bonna Rouse: back cover

Photographs:
Dreamstime: Peter Spirer: p. 27 (t), Jiri Castka: 31
Fotolia: p. 5 (t)
istockphoto.com: p. 18 (br), 21 (b)
Library of Congress: p. 20 (b), 24, 25
Shutterstock.com: front cover, title page, 4 (l), 5 (bl), 6, 7, 8, 9 (b), 10, 11, 14, 15, 16, 17, 19 (t), 22, 23, 30 (t & m); Andrey Bayda: p. 13; Dan Breckwoldt: p.19 (b); Andreas Klute: 27 (b); 3777190317: 28 (t); Denys Prykhodov: 28 (b); Darren Brode: 29
Thinkstock.com: title page, p. 12, 18 (bl), 20 (t), 21 (t), 26, 30 (b)

Every effort has been made to obtain the appropriate credit and full copyright clearance for all images in this book. Any oversights, despite Crabtree's greatest precautions, will be corrected in future editions.

Library and Archives Canada Cataloguing in Publication

Greil, Marlene
    United States : the land / Marlene Greil.

(The lands, peoples, and cultures series)
Includes index.
Issued also in electronic formats.
ISBN 978-0-7787-9835-4 (bound).--ISBN 978-0-7787-9838-5 (pbk.)

    1. United States--Description and travel--Juvenile literature.
I. Title. II. Series: Lands, peoples, and cultures series

E169.Z83G74 2012   j973   C2012-902721-9

Library of Congress Cataloging-in-Publication Data

Greil, Marlene.
    United States, the land / Marlene Greil.
      p. cm. -- (The lands, peoples, and cultures series)
"A Bobbie Kalman Book."
Includes an index.
    ISBN 978-0-7787-9835-4 (reinforced library binding : alk. paper) -- ISBN 978-0-7787-9838-5 (pbk. : alk. paper) -- ISBN 978-1-4271-7894-7 (electronic pdf.) -- ISBN 978-1-4271-8009-4 (electronic html.)
    1. United States--Geography--Juvenile literature. I. Title.

E161.3.G74 2012
917.3--dc23

2012016073

Crabtree Publishing Company
www.crabtreebooks.com   1-800-387-7650

Printed in Canada/102012/MA20120817

Published in Canada
Crabtree Publishing
616 Welland Ave.
St. Catharines, Ontario
L2M 5V6

Published in the United States
Crabtree Publishing
PMB 59051
350 Fifth Avenue, 59th Floor
New York, New York 10118

Published in the United Kingdom
Crabtree Publishing
Maritime House
Basin Road North, Hove
BN41 1WR

Published in Australia
Crabtree Publishing
3 Charles Street
Coburg North
VIC, 3058

Contents

In the Northeast region, the Cape Cod National Seashore is a protected area created in 1961 by President John F. Kennedy. It consists of 40 miles (64 km) of beaches, marshes, and ponds.

The United States is one of the largest countries in size in the world. One of the best ways to study the varied geography of this huge country is to look closely at its different geographic **regions.** A region's geography includes its **landforms** and bodies of water. The country's five main land regions are the Northeast, the Southeast, the Midwest, the Southwest, and the West. The states that make up each region have somewhat similar geographic features.

The Northeast is the smallest region in the United States, but what it lacks in size it makes up for in variety. This region includes the coastline of the Atlantic Ocean, the Coastal Plain, the Appalachian Mountains, two of the Great Lakes, and valleys and hills. The Southeast is diverse, too. Its inland areas are covered with mountains, hills, **plateaus,** and plains. With two coastlines, the Atlantic on the east and the Gulf of Mexico on the south, this region has **wetlands** such as the Everglades, which cover more than one million acres (404,686 hectares). As its name suggests, the Midwest region is located in the middle of the country. This is an area filled with lakes, including three Great Lakes, as well as

prairies and farmland. The Southwest region stretches from the Gulf of Mexico to the Colorado River and includes plains, plateaus, and mountains. The West, with its many mountains and peaks, has giant redwoods, rivers, deserts, and plateaus, and is where the highest and lowest land lies in the country.

(below) Plains and farmland can be seen for miles and miles across the Midwest.

Facts at a glance
Official name: The United States of America
Area: 3,794,083 square miles (9,826,630 square kilometers)
Population: Approximately 313,000,000
Capital: Washington, D.C.
Official language: English
Main religions: Christianity (Protestantism, Catholicism, other sects of Christianity), Judaism, Islam, Buddhism
Currency: U.S. dollar
Major holidays: New Year's Day, Memorial Day, Independence Day, Labor Day, Veterans Day, Thanksgiving Day, Christmas Day

The United States has 50 states and five regions: the Northeast, Southeast, Midwest, Southwest, and the West.

The Everglades, located in Florida in the Southeast region, covers more than one million acres (404,686 hectares). The largest subtropical wetland in the United States, the Everglades has plant and animal species found nowhere else in North America.

Ranching was one of the earliest industries in the Southwest and is still important today. Since much of the land is too dry for farming, beef cattle, sheep, and goats graze on this grassy land.

The vast land of the United States contains many kinds of landforms. Beginning in the east, flat lands stretch along the coast of the Atlantic Ocean from Massachusetts, south to the Gulf of Mexico. Just west of these coastal plains the land becomes higher as it reaches a chain of low mountains. The western edge of these mountains marks the beginning of the country's interior plains. The eastern part of the plains consists of flat and sometimes gently rolling land covered with grasses. Hills and plateaus lie within the interior plains. Farther west, the land rises to form high, rugged mountain ranges. Canyons, basins, and desert lowlands lie between these western mountains. Directly west is the long coast of the Pacific Ocean. Hawaii and Alaska, which are separated from the rest of the country, add even more variety to the American landscape.

How the United States was formed

Over thousands and thousands of years, natural processes shaped the landforms of the United States. Earth is made up of a group of tectonic plates. Some of the country's mountains were formed when two plates collided, pushing parts of Earth's crust higher and higher. Other high land was formed when hot magma deep inside Earth pushed up through cracks in its surface, creating volcanic mountains.

Over time, Earth experienced long periods of cold temperatures known as ice ages. During these times, ice covered the northern part of the United States. When temperatures warmed, large blocks of ice called glaciers broke off and began to move. As they moved, they flattened landforms and formed large basins. These basins often filled with water, creating lakes.

Topographical map of the United States

The Rocky Mountains, found along the western part of North America, make one of the longest mountain chains in the world. Some of the range's peaks rise more than 14,000 feet (4,267 m) above sea level.

Mountains

In both the east and the west, mountains rise up over the land of the United States. Two of the major ranges are the Appalachian Mountains in the east and the Rocky Mountains in the west.

The Appalachian Mountains stretch almost 2,000 miles (3,219 km) from the southern part of Canada to the middle of Alabama. They serve as a natural separation for the eastern Coastal Plain and the interior plains. Within the Appalachian chain are several mountain ranges including the Great Smoky, the Blue Ridge, the Catskills, and White Mountains. Mount Mitchell in the Blue Ridge area of North Carolina rises to 6,684 feet (2,037 m) and is the highest peak in the Appalachian Mountains. The Appalachians are the oldest mountains in the country. At one time, the peaks were high and pointed, but glaciers, wind, and rain have worn them down into rounded peaks. The Appalachians, with their many winding streams and rivers and no natural passes, presented many difficulties to early settlers and explorers heading west.

The Rocky Mountains extend from Canada to New Mexico for about 3,000 miles (4,828 km). They make up the largest and longest mountain range in the United States, and include smaller mountain ranges within them. The Rocky Mountains are younger than the Appalachian Mountains. This means that although the Rockies were formed millions of years ago, their peaks remain jagged and tall. The highest peak is Mount Elbert in Colorado, which rises to 14,440 feet (4,401 m). The Rockies were one of the last places in North America explored by Europeans because they are so rugged and difficult to cross.

The Great Plains

The land that lies near the center of the United States—west of the Appalachians and east of the Rockies—is called the interior plains. The western part of these massive plains is the Great Plains, which is one of the four major grasslands in the world. With few rivers and trees, this large dry and flat area includes parts of ten states—Texas, North Dakota, South Dakota, Montana, Nebraska, Wyoming, Colorado, Kansas, Oklahoma, and New Mexico. Even some parts of Canada are in the Great Plains. The land is diverse because the area of the Great Plains is so large. The Black Hills, the Missouri Plateau, the Colorado Piedmont, and Pecos Valley are all in the Great Plains.

Wheat has been a major crop of the Great Plains since the mid-1800s. Today this area is known as "America's breadbasket." This region is also home to ranchers, who raise cattle on the fertile grassland.

Named "the father of waters" by the Algonquian peoples, the Mississippi River is one of the longest rivers in the world. Here a barge transports products along the Mississippi in Louisiana.

Rivers

The United States has more than 250,000 rivers. The Mississippi, the Colorado, and the Rio Grande are three of the country's largest and most important rivers. The Mississippi River rises at its **source** in Minnesota and flows south through the middle of the United States about 2,350 miles (3,780 km) to the Gulf of Mexico. Once the steamboat made river transportation reliable, a large number of products were shipped by way of the Mississippi or one of its many **tributaries.** Two of these tributaries are the Ohio River and the Missouri River, which is one of the country's longest rivers. Today, products such as coal, steel, fertilizers, and grain move up and down the Mississippi. Tons of grain are carried to seaports, where it is exported to other countries.

The Colorado River is an important river in the Southwest. Much of the area is dry. Therefore, dams have been built to provide water for cities, industries, and agriculture and to help keep the river from flooding. The Hoover Dam crosses the Colorado River between Arizona and Nevada and is a major source of **hydroelectric power** for the area.

The Rio Grande River forms the border between Texas and the country of Mexico, and it meanders about 1,760 miles (2,830 km) from its source in the Rocky Mountains to the Gulf of Mexico. Along its route, it provides water for farming, serving as a source of irrigation for crops such as potatoes, alfalfa, cotton, pecans, and grapes.

The Great Lakes

The Great Lakes hold the largest supply of fresh water on Earth. Lake Superior, the largest, provides Duluth, Minnesota, with an international port. Lake Huron is the second largest of the Great Lakes and has the longest shoreline. Lake Michigan offers Chicago, Illinois, a gateway to the Mississippi River. Areas around Lake Erie have seen industrial growth because the lake's water is excellent for commerce, manufacturing, and power production. Lake Ontario provides a route for ships to pass through the St. Lawrence River and out into the Atlantic Ocean. Major **urban** industrial centers are found on the lake's shores because of this.

Lake Champlain, while not one of the Great Lakes, is the sixth largest body of fresh water in the United States. It serves as a link in the international waterway between New York City's harbor and the St. Lawrence Seaway.

(below) The St. Lawrence Seaway opened to navigation in 1959. It stretches 2,342 miles (3,769 km) from Duluth, Minnesota to the Atlantic Ocean.

The Sonoran Desert is the only place in the world where the saguaro cactus grows.

Western deserts

Deserts are formed by a lack of water and can be hot or cold. The Sonoran Desert is in the United States and Mexico and is one of the most beautiful deserts in the Americas. Although the Sonoran receives more rain than most deserts, its average rainfall each year is just 3 to 15 inches (75 to 380 mm). This rain occurs during its two wet seasons from December through March and from July through September. There are three other deserts in North America: the Mojave in southwestern Utah, Nevada, and eastern California; the Chihuahuan in southeastern New Mexico and western Texas in the United States and in Mexico; and the Great Basin in parts of Nevada, Utah, Idaho, and Oregon. Like the Sonoran, the Mojave and Chihuahuan are hot deserts because they have high temperatures during the summer. The Great Basin is a cold desert.

No place on Earth is drier than a desert, and the driest and hottest place in North America is Death Valley in the Mojave Desert. Death Valley receives fewer than 2 inches (50 mm) of rainfall each year and has reached high temperatures of 134° F (57° C). It has the lowest elevation, too, at 282 feet (86 m) below sea level. Death Valley's rock formations were shaped by erosion, the wearing away of Earth's surface, and its craters were shaped by volcanic activity.

Western landforms

Canyons are deep, narrow valleys with steep sides that are formed over time. For example, the Grand Canyon was shaped over millions of years by water and wind erosion and other environmental conditions. Over time, the waters of the Colorado River wore away rocks, creating the present-day geographic wonder.

Another type of canyon, a slot canyon, begins as a small crack in rock that is acted on by rapidly flowing water. Eventually, erosion forms a deep crevice. About a thousand slot canyons are in Utah because of the state's eroding soft sandstone and dry conditions. One of the most well-known slot canyons is Zion Canyon.

(below) Water erosion from the Virgin River carved Zion Canyon, which today is about 15 miles (25 km) long and about 3,000 feet (914 m) deep.

Coastal regions—the Northeast and Southeast

States that border the Atlantic Ocean have always been centers of fishing and shipping industries. The Atlantic Ocean provides a supply of fish, oysters, and lobsters. With 13 states bordering the Atlantic Ocean, this region provides many ports for trade throughout the United States and internationally. In addition, it is a starting point for many cruise ships. The eastern coastal region also has big cities and beach towns. Places such as Cape Cod, Massachusetts, Myrtle Beach, South Carolina, and islands off the Georgia and North Carolina coasts draw tourists from throughout the world.

Coastal regions—the Gulf Coast

States along the Gulf Coast are Florida, Alabama, Mississippi, Louisiana, and Texas. This area has beaches, golf courses, and theme parks, which attract many tourists to these states. The area is also the location of the United States Space and Rocket Center in Huntsville, Alabama, and the Kennedy Space Center in Cape Canaveral, Florida. The Gulf Coast has fertile soil and many rivers, so fishing and farming are important. After major discoveries of oil in Texas and the waters of the Gulf of Mexico, the oil **industry** boomed, bringing major national and international companies to the area.

Coastal regions—the West

The western coastline stretches from southern California through Oregon, Washington, and Alaska, and includes Hawaii. Los Angeles and San Francisco in California, and Seattle in Washington, are three major ports, providing sea transportation for products heading to countries to the west. These areas are also known for fishing and tourism. Alaska is a major location for fishing. Oil is the second main industry in Alaska, which is well equipped for transporting it through the state's many miles (km) of pipelines. Hawaii lies in the middle of the Pacific and is a favorite tourist destination because of its beaches and other scenic wonders.

Visitors to Oregon's beaches can enjoy warm temperatures in September and early October and may even spot whales swimming just off the coast.

Climate

Regional climates

The United States is so large that types of weather and **climates** differ from place to place. The winter climate in the Northeast is usually cold and snowy with a threat of blizzards, which are severe snowstorms with high winds. Spring is warm and sunny, and summer is hot and can be rainy. Autumn brings cool weather.

The Southeast usually has hot and humid summers and warm, wet, and sunny winters. It also has the possibility of **hurricanes** between June and November. Hurricanes form over warm ocean waters and move over land. When they make landfall, hurricanes cause severe damage.

During the summer, the Midwest region's climate is hot and rainy and during the winter, it is snowy and cold. The Midwest has winter blizzards and spring and summer thunderstorms, which produce **tornadoes.**

The Southwest region has a mostly hot and dry climate, but mountain locations can be cold and snowy.

(left) Wind speeds from tornadoes can reach more than 250 miles (402 km) per hour, and the path of damage can be as great as 50 miles (80 km) long.

The most diverse climate is in the West. Hawaii is warm and tropical, while Alaska is frigid. The West has the hottest, coldest, and rainiest places. Death Valley once had a high temperature of 134° F (56.7° C) and Prospect Creek Camp, Alaska, had a low temperature of –80° F (–62° C). Mount Waialeale, Hawaii, has an average of 460 inches (11,684 mm) of rain a year. The snowiest region is found here too, in the Cascade Mountains of Washington. The West has natural disasters such as earthquakes and volcanoes.

Flooding and fires

All parts of the United States can flood and that makes flooding the number one disaster in the country. Hurricanes, blizzards, melting snow, and heavy rains are all causes of floods.

Wildfires commonly occur in forest areas in the Southeast, Southwest, and West. Caused by drought conditions, lightning, arson, or carelessness, these fires scorch millions of acres (hectares) of land.

During the spring and summer of 2011, floods occurred in more than 15 states causing loss of life and destruction to homes and land.

People

While people of many different heritages live in the United States, they are not evenly distributed. The country's distribution of people today can be traced back to the settlement patterns of their ancestors.

Waterways affect settlement

Rivers allowed Native Americans to populate many places in North America. Later, improved shipbuilding helped Europeans cross the Atlantic Ocean. Spanish explorers sailed to the southern areas of the continent, and the Spanish eventually established settlements in Mexico. The western United States has a stronger Spanish influence because of this. The English headed farther north, eventually establishing 13 colonies along the eastern coast. The Atlantic Ocean also carried ships holding enslaved Africans to both Spanish- and English-controlled lands. After the American colonists gained independence, river travel helped settlers move west. Settlements often began near rivers, which were used as a source of water, for transportation, and for fishing.

Land and climate play a role

The flat land of the Atlantic coast proved good for growing crops. Fertile land and a mild climate meant that some colonists in the Southeast could establish large farms. Their main crop—cotton—required hard work, and colonists brought over more African slave labor. At first, the Appalachian Mountains blocked settlers from moving west. Then they found a way to pass through the mountains and venture into western territories. Some of the high, cold, and dry lands, however, proved harder for settlement and farming.

Each year on July 4, people of many cultures join together to celebrate American independence.

Visitors to San Francisco's Chinatown have a chance to experience Asian foods and cultures. Signs written in the Chinese language are common sights.

Interaction of cultures

The encounters of Native Americans, Europeans, and Africans brought about an exchange of products, foods, and ideas. Native Americans had never seen horses or guns before. Europeans were delighted to taste such foods as tomatoes, corn, beans, and potatoes. Enslaved Africans brought African music, traditions, and recipes.

Immigration adds diversity

Since the country's earliest days, **immigrants** from other parts of the world have come seeking new beginnings. The blending of various heritages has helped create a unique American culture.

Early immigrants

The first American colonists sailed from Europe for a variety of reasons. Spanish colonists came in search of precious metals such as gold. English colonists known as Pilgrims headed for Massachusetts to practice their religion freely. Colonists in Virginia, New York, and North Carolina had the goal of making money. Many debtors came to Georgia in search of better lives. The east coast of North America became home to Dutch, German, French, Swedish, Irish, and Scottish settlers as well. Unlike the European immigrants who chose to settle in North America, Africans were enslaved and forced to move to the distant continent.

Immigration in the 1800s and early 1900s

Immigration to the United States continued after the country gained its independence. Millions of Irish came to escape famine and hard times. The Gold Rush in California brought Chinese workers. Later, many Italians entered the United States, heading to the cities of the northeast. Jewish people from eastern Europe came seeking relief from religious mistreatment.

People within the United States relocated as well. Many African Americans in the Southeast moved to northern cities for jobs in factories and improved ways of life.

Modern-day immigration

Immigration continues today, but now more people come from Latin America and Asia than from Europe. A large number of Cubans fled their island nation to enjoy more freedoms in a democratic nation. Many Mexicans have traveled north for jobs and better lives for their children. The need to escape from war brought immigrants from Vietnam and other Asian countries. People of different cultures bring their customs, foods, ideas, and music.

Washington, D.C.

For more than 200 years, Washington, D.C., has served as the center of national government for the United States. The city's location was carefully planned to be at the center of the 13 original states that made up the newly-formed country. Architect Pierre L'Enfant had grand plans when he designed the new capital city. Benjamin Banneker, an African American, helped survey the land of the future city. Today, lawmakers meet in the city to make decisions that affect citizens throughout the nation. In addition, the historic treasures of the nation's capital attract millions of visitors every year.

The Capitol

The country's legislative branch, or Congress, meets in Washington, D.C., in the United States Capitol. Congress is made up of two parts, the Senate and the House of Representatives. Each has its own meeting chamber in the Capitol. Tourists to the building can watch Congress while it is in session.

Built of Virginia sandstone painted white, the White House is large and impressive, with 132 rooms and 35 bathrooms. It even has its own theater, bowling alley, and swimming pool.

The White House

The president of the United States lives and works at the White House, located at 1600 Pennsylvania Avenue in Washington, D.C. Built more than 200 years ago, the White House has been home to every president since John Adams, the second president.

The West Wing of the White House is the headquarters of the executive branch of government, led by the president. The West Wing holds the president's personal office called the Oval Office. Nearby is the Cabinet Room where the president meets with advisors. From this room, the beautiful Rose Garden can be viewed. The presidential family lives on the second floor of the part of the White House known as the Residence. On the first floor, the president welcomes guests in the Blue Room and hosts dinners for up to 140 guests in the State Dining Room.

The United States Capitol is built in the neoclassical style, with many ancient Greek and Roman influences. The Capitol's impressive dome makes it immediately recognizable.

The Smithsonian Institution

At the center of Washington, D.C., is the park known as the National Mall. Facing the mall are government and cultural buildings including the series of museums that are part of the Smithsonian Institution. The Museum of American History features artifacts of the country's past such as gowns of First Ladies. At the Air and Space Museum, artifacts from early airplanes to space shuttles and beyond can be seen. The Museum of the American Indian pays tribute to Native Americans, the first peoples of North America. Highlights of the Natural History Museum are a large African elephant and the Hope Diamond. The nation's art takes center stage at the American Art Museum and the Portrait Gallery. Away from the mall, children enjoy spending the day at the National Zoo, where giant pandas, tigers, and other animals live in natural surroundings.

Monuments

Throughout Washington, D.C., monuments and memorials honor people and events of the past. The towering **landmark** known as the Washington Monument honors the country's first president, George Washington. A highlight of the Lincoln Memorial is a huge statue of Abraham Lincoln, who led the country through

Millions of tourists come to the National Mall every year to visit its monuments and memorials, festivals, and the museums that surround it. In spring, thousands of beautiful cherry trees can be seen in full bloom.

the Civil War. The Jefferson Memorial features a dome and columns in the style favored by the country's third president, Thomas Jefferson, who wrote the Declaration of Independence and was a talented architect himself. At the Martin Luther King, Jr., Memorial, visitors pay respect to the slain civil rights leader. Those who fought for democracy are honored at the Vietnam Veterans Memorial, the Vietnam Women's Memorial, the Korean War Memorial, and the National World War II Memorial.

(below) The capital city's tallest structure, the Washington Monument, can be seen high above other sites at the National Mall and in the Reflecting Pond.

Many of America's cities rose from settlements founded by Native Americans or Europeans, including English, Dutch, and Spanish colonists. Today, new and old combine to create vibrant cities across the five regions of the United States. Alongside historic churches and homes stand sprawling factories and towering skyscrapers. Across the United States, almost 80 percent of all Americans call urban areas home.

Boston

Boston traces its roots to a group of settlers from England called the Puritans, who traveled to North America to practice their religion freely. In the mid-1700s, Bostonians such as Patrick Henry urged American colonists to break away and form an independent United States. In the 1800s and 1900s, people from around the world, including many Irish, immigrated to Boston. As the capital of Massachusetts, the city is the seat of government for the state. It is also a thriving seaport; financial, medical, and technology center; and tourist destination.

Thousands of people board the elevators at the Empire State Building daily to ride more than 1,000 feet (305 m) up for a dramatic view of the landscape of New York City.

New York City

New York City rose up at the mouth of the Hudson River. Its earliest residents were Native Americans. In 1624, Dutch colonists built a settlement there called New Amsterdam. Just 40 years later, the English claimed it, renaming it New York. From then on, the city grew steadily, with immigrants arriving from Europe, Asia, South America, and Africa.

(left) The historic Old North Church still stands in the North End neighborhood of Boston. It was from this church that a friend signaled to Paul Revere that British troops were going by sea to the towns of Lexington and Concord. The American patriot immediately jumped on his horse, shouting out a warning. This was just one role Bostonians played in the events before and during the American Revolution.

New York City is divided into five smaller parts called boroughs: Manhattan, Brooklyn, Queens, Bronx, and Staten Island. Manhattan's Wall Street district is a center of financial activity for the city and entire country. The city is also a well-known cultural center. Tourists and New Yorkers alike visit the city's museums such as the Metropolitan Museum of Art and historic landmarks such as the Empire State Building and the Statue of Liberty. Among the city's busy streets and **skyscrapers** are areas of green space, including Central Park.

Miami

At the start of the twentieth century, Miami was just a small town in southern Florida. Over the years, many people have been drawn to Miami to live or visit because of its warm climate. Tourists flock to Miami's beaches in winter. Many retired people make a permanent move to Miami and other parts of Florida because of its pleasant climate. About 2.5 million people now live in the area in and around Miami.

Today Miami is known as the gateway to South America and the countries of the Caribbean because of its location close to those regions. Miami has attracted immigrants from countries to its south, particularly Cuba, who have come in search of a better life. Because of this, Miami

Cruise ships are a common sight at the Port of Miami, which welcomes about 4 million tourists a year. In addition, ships carry cargo to and from more than 250 ports around the world each year.

is heavily influenced by Hispanic culture, and both English and Spanish are commonly spoken. Today, Miami is truly a **multicultural** city.

Atlanta

Transportation gave birth to the city of Atlanta, which began in the 1830s at the end of a railroad line. Today, Atlanta, Georgia, is known as a transportation hub for the United States and all parts of the world. Its airport, Hartsfield-Jackson Atlanta International Airport, is one of the nation's busiest.

The ever-growing city of Atlanta boasts a large number of eye-catching skyscrapers.

Atlanta is one of the most important cities in the Southeast. It is a key banking center and home to many national and international businesses. Atlanta also boasts many cultural attractions including a symphony, an opera, theaters, art and history museums, and an aquarium.

Chicago

After settling much of the east, Americans began to push west. In the mid-1700s, a free black trader named Jean Baptiste Point du Sable became the first person to settle the land now known as Chicago in the Midwest. By the 1860s, Chicago, Illinois, had grown into a small city supported by trade. The Great Chicago Fire of 1871 destroyed much of the city, but residents quickly began rebuilding. Brick and stone buildings, including early skyscrapers, rose from the ashes of the old city.

The railroad and the meat-packing industries helped Chicago grow. Its location near railroad lines and along Lake Michigan made it a major transportation and commerce center for the Midwest. Many European immigrants settled in Chicago to work in its bustling factories. Today, Chicago has a very diverse population,

including people of African, Asian, and Hispanic heritage. In the twenty-first century, the city remains a bustling transportation, industrial, and cultural center.

Dallas

American pioneers moved farther and farther west, settling the land. The small settlement of Dallas was just a few years old when Texas officially became a part of the United States. Dallas's population grew greatly as many Southerners moved there to rebuild their lives after the Civil War.

As communication and transportation improved, Dallas became a shipping point for goods such as grains and cattle. The discovery of oil not far from Dallas brought more wealth to the city. It is now a leader in the fields of technology, finance, transportation, and telecommunications.

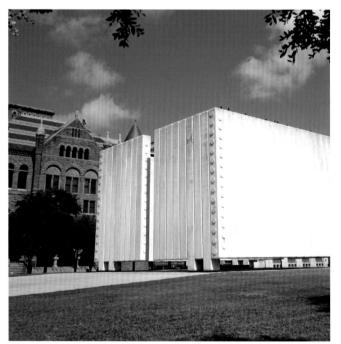

(above) In downtown Dallas, the John F. Kennedy Memorial Plaza honors the assassinated president. Beside the plaza is a historic red sandstone courthouse.

(left) Chicagoans find many recreational activities at downtown Grant Park, which faces Lake Michigan. Towering over the park is the Willis Tower, the tallest skyscraper in the United States.

Seattle

In the mid-1850s, settlers set down roots along a waterway called Puget Sound in what would become the state of Washington. The early residents of Seattle depended on lumber, shipbuilding, fishing, and trade to earn their living. Shipbuilding and lumber are still important to Seattle, but the city is also an important **producer** of airplanes and technology products. In their leisure time, the people of Seattle enjoy the natural beauty of the land and take part in a wide variety of cultural and sports activities.

Los Angeles

In the mid-1700s, the Spanish arrived from their territories in what is now Mexico to claim land in California, and the city of Los Angeles grew from a small Spanish settlement. Many Spanish influences can still be seen throughout the city because of this. Today, structures in Los Angeles are designed to withstand earthquakes. Mention Los Angeles to most people, and Hollywood immediately comes to mind. Movie making is a main industry in Los Angeles. So too is tourism, with visitors flocking to movie studies, the beaches, and amusement parks in or around the city.

(above) The structure known as the Space Needle rises above the skyline of Seattle. Built for the 1962 World's Fair, the Space Needle remains an important tourist attraction, with spectacular views from its observation deck.

(below) Positioned high on Mount Lee in Los Angeles, the letters that spell out the name Hollywood announce to the world that the city hosts the world's most famous movie studios.

Historic sites and national parks

America's natural beauty is **preserved** in its national parks. Since the creation of Yellowstone National Park in 1872, the country's national parks have grown to nearly 400. President Theodore Roosevelt, known for his love of nature, established five national parks and four national monuments during his presidency. National parks and monuments provide a way to keep natural and historic landmarks and native plants and animals safe from harm. They also offer people recreational opportunities and a chance to observe the country's natural wonders.

Mount Rushmore

In 1934, Gutzon Borglum began a massive carving of four presidents in the Black Hills of South Dakota. Each year, millions of visitors come to what is now Mount Rushmore National Memorial to see this symbol of freedom. In addition to safeguarding this national treasure, the park protects certain species of goats, vultures, frogs, wildflowers, and Ponderosa pine trees.

Images of George Washington, Thomas Jefferson, Theodore Roosevelt, and Abraham Lincoln are carved into a granite rock formation at Mount Rushmore.

(above right) Old Faithful is the most famous of Yellowstone's more than 10,000 natural water features. Old Faithful gained its name because it regularly erupts many times throughout the day.

Yellowstone

This large park stretches through parts of Montana, Wyoming, and Idaho. Best known among the natural features of the park are its hot springs and geysers, including Old Faithful. Yellowstone is the only place in the United States where bison, sometimes called buffalo, have lived continuously for thousands of years. Also protected are grizzly bears, bobcats, gophers, moose, and the Yellowstone sand verbena plant, found nowhere else in the world.

Yosemite

Powerful waterfalls are a highlight of any visit to Yosemite National Park in California. Those ready for adventure try to climb the granite cliffs of Half Dome. Tourists also discover that the park showcases and protects mountains, valleys, forests, and a variety of plants and animals. Since one purpose of the national park system is to ensure that Yosemite keeps its environment close to its natural state, animals such as mule deer, coyote, and black bear live much as they always have.

A caribou pauses near the mountain named Denali by the native people of Alaska.

Denali

Located in Alaska, Denali National Park & Preserve was established to protect the area's natural and cultural resources. One of the main reasons for the park's creation was to protect the animals that live in the area, including bull moose, caribou, grizzly bears, and Dall sheep. The park is a safe haven for more than 650 kinds of flowering plants, as well as many species of lichens and moss, that can survive in an extremely cold climate. The park also protects its landscape featuring Mt. McKinley, or Denali, and other high, snowy mountains. At the same time, it offers once-in-a-lifetime opportunities for visitors to ski and mountain climb. In addition, the park protects the history and cultures of the people who have called this frozen area home.

Hawaii's parks

Far from the freezing cold of Alaska lie the islands that make up the warm and sunny state of Hawaii. Its national parks give visitors a close-up look at the state's history, culture, and plant and animal life. Pu'uhonua o Hōnaunau preserves temples and homes of historic villages. At Hawai`i Volcanoes National Park, visitors can see craters from extinct volcanoes and steam from active lava flows. Waterfalls and a tropical rainforest are just two attractions at Haleakala National Park.

Spanish missions

Arizona's Tumacácori National Historical Park is a good place to learn about the Spanish heritage of the American Southwest. Visitors can see the ruins of three Spanish missions from which Jesuit priests spread Christianity. The park is also known for its forest of mesquite trees. Local native people once used mesquite wood as firewood, and ate the beans produced by the trees.

The ruins of Spanish missions can be found at Tumacácori National Historical Park, south of Tucson, Arizona.

Both the land and water of the United States provide food and employment for millions of people. More than 2.2 million farms in the country produce crops including corn, soybeans, wheat, sugarcane, fruits, cotton, and vegetables. Many farms sell poultry, eggs, milk, and other dairy products. Cattle production is one of the nation's most important industries. The east and west coast waters, as well as the waters of the Gulf of Mexico, support the nation's important fishing industry.

Crops

Throughout much of the Midwest in what is referred to as the "Corn Belt," farmers produce about 40 percent of the world's corn. This makes the United States the world's largest producer of this crop. In the past, it took weeks to harvest corn because it was done by hand. Today, a machine called a combine harvests acres of corn in several minutes. More than half of the corn is used to feed livestock throughout the world. The rest is used for food products and in industry.

Sugar refineries are factories that prepare and change sugarcane into sugar, which is an important ingredient in food. Sugar is sucrose, a natural carbohydrate that is found in fruits and vegetables. It is easier to obtain sucrose from sugarcane and sugar beets than from other plants.

Soybeans are the second largest crop in the United States, and the country is the leading soybean producer in the world. Most soybeans are grown in the Midwest and then exported to more than 80 countries worldwide. Soybeans are processed for oil, which can be used in cooking, for diesel fuel, or for industrial uses. Soybeans are used in feed for livestock, too. The Midwest is also a major producer of wheat, most of which is used to make flour. That is why the Midwest has another nickname, "America's breadbasket."

Another important crop is sugarcane, which is grown mainly in Florida, Louisiana, Texas, and Hawaii. Separating sugar from the sugarcane plant involves turning sugarcane into raw sugar, which is done at sugar mills, and then sending it to refineries that produce sugar as we know it.

(left) Today, with the help of new farming methods, technology, and hybrid corn, farmers grow more corn on less land than they did about 75 years ago. Hybrid corn comes from the grain of one corn being mixed with other types. Hybrid corn is larger and provides more corn with each crop.

The cow on the left is a Hereford, a meat cow. The cow on the right is a Holstein-Friesian, a milk cow. Although females from all breeds of cattle produce milk and meat, some breeds are better suited for milk and others for meat.

Livestock

Cattle graze on open land and pastures in many parts of the United States, with a high number found in the Great Plains, the West, and the Southwest. Some cattle ranches or farms are family run, and more farms in the United States raise beef cattle than any other type of product. Beef cattle provide meat. Breeds of beef cattle came to the United States during the 1500s. Two types of beef cows are Hereford cows, which originated in Herefordshire, England, and Angus cows, which came from northern Scotland.

In the Northeast, Southeast, Central Plains of the Midwest, and West, many farmers raise dairy cows. Dairy cows provide milk, which is used for cheese, butter, yogurt, ice cream, and other dairy products. These are foods consumed by most Americans. Different dairy cows provide different milk products. A popular breed of cow is the Holstein-Friesian cow. These cows are usually black and white, and they are known for producing more milk than other breeds.

Fisheries

Fishing is a major industry in the United States. From "sea to shining sea," the country's numerous bodies of water hold large amounts of seafood. In the Northeast and Southeast, the Atlantic Ocean's coastal waters provide fish, oysters, clams, lobsters, and crabs. In the West,

the Pacific Ocean's coastal waters contain fish and shellfish such as salmon, tuna, oysters, and clams. Along the Gulf of Mexico, fishers catch shrimp, crabs, oysters, red snapper, and tuna. The Gulf area is the location of eight of the major fishing ports in the country based on dollar value. Freshwater fish are also found in the nation's many lakes and rivers, especially those in the Northeast, Southeast, and Midwest regions.

New Bedford, Massachusetts, the "Whaling City," is the number one fishing port in the country. Although its success was once connected to whaling ships, it is now largely due to scallops, which are exported to many places including Belgium, France, and Canada.

Beginnings of industry

The **Industrial Revolution** began in Great Britain in the 1780s and quickly spread to the United States. This period of time was truly a revolution because it completely changed how people lived and worked. People began to use machines to do work quickly that had always been done slowly by hand. In the United States, the textile, or cloth, industry was the first to modernize. Textiles mills used water power from nearby rivers to run machines that spun thread and wove cloth. Many of the new jobs in the mills were filled by women and children.

Throughout much of the 1800s and early 1900s, people and inventors continued to make improvements in industry. As more and more factories opened in cities, Americans moved there from homes in the countryside.

Andrew Carnegie

One child worker in a textile factory grew up to be a leader of industry. Of Scottish heritage, Andrew Carnegie grew up in Pittsburgh, Pennsylvania. There he founded Carnegie Steel. His company made steel for railroads and skyscrapers and grew to become one the nation's largest. Carnegie put his wealth to use by donating much of it to libraries and schools.

Thomas Edison

Thomas Edison's many inventions helped improve the world. His work with electricity earned him the nickname "Wizard of Menlo Park," where he had a laboratory. His **phonograph** brought music into American homes. His motion picture camera helped pave the way for the movie industry.

Carnegie's steel mills were located near railroads so that steel products could be easily transported to cities.

His most important work, however, was his development of an electric lightbulb that did not burn out quickly. Through his efforts, whole cities were soon powered by electricity.

Alexander Graham Bell

Born in Scotland, Alexander Graham Bell's work on the telephone changed **communication** in the world forever. His study of hearing and speech led him to invent a practical telephone. Later, in Boston, he started the first telephone company to relay the human voice over long distances. His 1876 invention led to the development of smart phones and **fiber optics**.

Henry Ford

In much the same way that Alexander Graham Bell changed communication, Henry Ford changed transportation. Like several other inventors of his time, Henry Ford developed a self-powered vehicle. Unlike other inventors, Ford found ways to make automobiles available to a large number of Americans. His Model-T, developed in the early 1900s, was both well built and well priced. Using conveyor belts, **assembly lines,** and standardized parts, the Ford Motor Company was able to **mass produce** cars, which the public quickly bought and took on the road. Ford's work helped make Michigan the automobile capital of the United States.

The Wright brothers

Air travel took flight through the imagination and experiments of Wilbur and Orville Wright. The Wright brothers were making and selling bicycles in Dayton, Ohio, when they began experiments building flying machines. By 1903, the brothers were ready to give flight to a heavier-than-air flying machine. In Kitty Hawk, North Carolina, the Wrights successfully flew a powered airplane. This event marked the start of air and space travel.

(right) The Wright Flyer successfully lifts off the ground and makes a short flight.

Workers build Model-Ts on an assembly line.

George Washington Carver

While machinery was revolutionizing the way food was processed, George Washington Carver was revolutionizing food itself. Born a slave in Missouri in 1864, he persevered in pursuing higher education at a time when any education was often denied to African Americans. This scientist, botanist, and inventor brought life back to American agriculture after the devastating crop failures in the United States during the 1930s. Carver's method of crop rotation and his invention of more than 300 peanut-based products helped move agriculture into a new era.

Over the years, the United States has experienced many changes in transportation. Always on the lookout to travel farther and faster, Americans developed new ways to move themselves and products from place to place. These advances have led to a strong and efficient system of transportation that offers people access to goods, services, entertainment, jobs, and each other.

Roads and highways

One of the first advances in road building came about because of the need to transport goods to settlers west of the Appalachian Mountains. In the early 1800s, Congress authorized the building of a National Road from Maryland to what would soon become the state of Ohio. More roads in other parts of the country followed. During the Great Depression in the 1930s, the government put people to work building and repairing United States highways.

Today, multi-lane interstate highways take people and products across state lines on almost 50,000 miles (80,467 km) of road. Toll roads called turnpikes run through many states, and circular beltways surround many cities. Millions of vehicles including cars, trucks, taxis, and buses travel American roads daily.

Waterways

Long ago, Americans used the country's rivers for travel and for trade. In fact, they built water routes called canals to help them get from place to place. In the twenty-first century, the country's rivers are used mostly for recreation and for the transportation of **cargo**. More than half of the country's grain exports are transported down the Mississippi River to ports on the Gulf of Mexico. Ports in Louisiana, Texas, California, and other states are busy centers of trade, with more than two million tons of cargo passing through them. Exports include wheat and

Fruits and vegetables are among the many goods shipped by truck to places across the nation.

Over 4.3 million New Yorkers use the subway each day.

soybeans, coal, **petroleum,** and iron ore. Ports in Florida, including the Port of Miami, are among the world's busiest cruise ports.

Trains and railroads

The development of a practical steam engine by English inventor James Watt set the stage for a network of railroads in the United States. Steam trains sped along railroad lines in Baltimore and Ohio. The completion of a **transcontinental railroad** in 1869 enabled people and products to travel from coast to coast. Modern-day trains carry more than two-fifths of the country's freight, including vegetables, grain, coal, lumber, chemicals, and metals. Amtrak and other trains take passengers from city to city and state to state. Subways and light rail move people from place to place within cities. New kinds of high-speed passenger rail are being planned as a way to overcome increasing traffic on roads and highways.

Los Angeles International Airport is one of the world's busiest airports. Thousands of flights take off every day, and more than 60 million passengers use the airport each year.

Air travel

After the Wright brothers' flight, Americans became enchanted with the idea of flying. Americans cheered in 1927 when Charles Lindbergh flew across the Atlantic in the *Spirit of St. Louis*. Since then, airplanes have become an important way for people in the United States to travel long distances quickly. Some of the nation's busiest airports are located in Atlanta, Chicago, Dallas-Fort Worth, Denver, and Los Angeles. The country's advances in flight might even amaze the Wright brothers. Americans have been to the moon, traveled on space shuttles, and lived and worked for months on the **International Space Station.**

Industry today

Since the early 1900s, industry in the United States has undergone many changes. Workers in agriculture and manufacturing no longer represent the majority. Instead, about 78 percent of the workforce makes its living in **service industries.** Many others work in professional or technology-related fields.

Technology

Silicon Valley, located in the San Francisco Bay area in northern California, is the birthplace of the **microprocessor** and other electronic innovations. Companies such as Hewlett-Packard, Intel, Dell, and Google are part of Silicon Valley. Apple, which began when Steve Wozniak and Steve Jobs built their first computer in Jobs's garage, is also part of the Silicon Valley culture. Since its beginning, Apple has offered leading-edge electronic products that are simple to use. Over the years, these have included the Apple I and II, Macintosh, iMac, iPod, iPhone, and iPad. Each product changed the electronics industry and how people work, study, and play.

Steve Jobs, co-founder of Apple, was responsible for inventions that enabled people to own personal computers and access the Internet from their homes. He changed the way people listen to and buy music and the way they think about and use phones.

(below) Bill Gates, co-founder of Microsoft, has made a difference with more than his inventions. He and his wife spend much of their time supporting and funding research to find cures for diseases such as AIDS and to solve some of the other serious problems facing people throughout the world.

Bill Gates and Paul Allen began Microsoft in New Mexico. They eventually moved to Washington. In the 1970s, they created MS-DOS, an operating system for IBM personal computers. In 1995, Microsoft introduced Windows 95. Today, millions of personal computers use some version of Windows as well as Microsoft software for word processing, spreadsheets, games, and other applications.

Just as entrepreneurs Jobs and Gates changed the technology industry, Mark Zuckerberg, founder of Facebook, changed the way people communicate. He founded Facebook in 2004 and since that time, more than 500 million people have created their own Facebook pages to share photos, experiences, and many other facts about their lives.

Automotive industry

Many changes have taken place in the automotive industry in the United States since Henry Ford first made the Model-T. The United States is a nation of car buyers. Meeting the need for new cars are at least 12 manufacturing companies including General Motors, Ford, and Chrysler. European, Japanese, and Korean manufacturers also produce vehicles in the United States. American manufacturers are building more plants and adapting existing ones to build hybrid and electric cars. Manufacturers are also adding "green" features to new and updated models.

Medicine

Before Jonas Salk discovered a vaccine in 1955 to protect children from polio, thousands of children were infected with this virus every year. Polio is an illness that may cause a person to lose his or her ability to move. In places where Salk's vaccination is used, the disease has been almost completely eliminated. Medical research has continued growing in importance since the 1950s. Many pharmaceutical, or drug, companies conduct research hoping to find new medicines to treat or cure diseases.

Tourism

Throughout the United States, people work in the tourism industry at hotels, restaurants, museums, and other places that serve people. Millions of people from all over the world visit places in the United States, and tourism is a major industry. Beaches attract visitors from near and far. Many people come to play golf, fish, and ski, or visit monuments, historic sites, theme parks, and national parks. Others are attracted to areas for their cultural activities. America's most popular destinations include New York City; Disney World in Florida; Disneyland in California; Niagara Falls, New York; and Great Smoky National Park in Tennessee and North Carolina.

The U.S. automotive industry is becoming more competitive with foreign car manufacturers. A writer for Automobile Magazine *recently said about the 2012 Ford Fusion Hybrid, "Overall I'd say this is the best mid-size hybrid you can buy."*

People in the United States have always relied on nature. At times, this reliance has led humans to destroy wildlife, clear forests, overuse water, pollute the air, and do other damage to nature. It has, however, also led humans to **conserve** the nation's natural resources, preserve and protect flora and fauna, and control pollution.

Natural resources and alternatives

Natural resources include water, trees, and soil. They also include resources under the ground such as minerals and fuels. Minerals are found in rocks and include copper, gold, silver, iron, marble, and limestone. People use these minerals to make coins, jewelry, and in construction. They use fuels such as oil, natural gas, and coal to create heat and energy. Minerals and fuels are nonrenewable resources. This means that once they are used up, they cannot be replaced. That is why it is important for people to conserve natural resources. People can conserve by using less and by recycling.

Natural resources are things found in nature such as minerals, water, or soil that people use to meet their needs.

People can also use renewable energy sources, or sources that can be made again by people or by nature. These include wind power (energy from moving air), solar power (energy from the sun), biomass (energy from plants and animals), hydropower (energy from moving water), and geothermal energy (heat from inside Earth). Only about one-tenth of electricity comes from these renewable sources.

Alternative energy forms include (top left) wind power, (top right) solar panels, (bottom left) hydropower, and (bottom right) geothermal.

Examples of endangered/threatened plants and animals		
Name	**Description**	**Where Found**
Rare orchid, *Platanthera holochila*	endangered	Kokee State Park in Hawaii
American hart's tongue fern	threatened	Hiawatha National Forest in Michigan
Arizona hedgehog cactus	endangered	Tonto National Forest and Agua Fria National Monument in Arizona
Blue whale	endangered	Hawaii and Pacific coast states, including Alaska
'Ua'u (seabirds)	endangered	Haleakala National Park in Hawaii
American bison	vulnerable (may be in danger)	Yellowstone National Park and other national parks

Yet even this amount lessens the demand for other fuels and helps the environment. As cheaper ways to produce renewable fuels are found, their use will grow. Geothermal power plants already provide California with almost five percent of its electricity, and within the next ten years this may double.

Preserve and protect nature
National parks in the United States provide habitats for many endangered or threatened species of flora and fauna. Flora and fauna are groups of plants and wildlife, respectively, that live in a specific region. They may become endangered or threatened for several different reasons. They may lose their habitat or their environment may become contaminated. They may have too much competition from non-native species or be collected and sold for commercial use.

Pollution
Pollution causes natural resources to become dirty and unsafe for use. It can be in the air, in water, or on the land. Causes of pollution include hazardous materials such as smoke, pesticides, and oil. Chemicals from industry, cars, and homes entering the air, water, or land are also sources of pollution. Recycling, reusing, avoiding harmful products, disposing of chemicals properly, and picking up litter are some ways to reduce pollution. Renewable energy sources may also reduce pollution because they offer a clean option to oil, natural gas, and coal.

The black-footed ferret is one of the most endangered land animals in North America and is the continent's only native ferret. A member of the weasel family, this mammal uses a burrow for shelter. It was reintroduced in 1994 into Badlands National Park in South Dakota.

 # Glossary

assembly lines Arrangement of machines and workers so that work passes from one to the next in a direct line until products are assembled and finished

cargo Goods transported by airplane, ship, train, or truck

climate The pattern of weather in a certain area over a long period of time

communication Ways to share information or feelings with others

conserve To prevent something from being harmed, used up, or wasted

deserts Regions that are dry and receive very little rainfall each year

fiber optics Bundles of glass fibers that send large amounts of information quickly, as bursts of light

hurricanes Violent, powerful tropical storms that have strong winds and heavy rain

hydroelectric power Electricity that is generated by the power of moving water

immigrants People who settle in another country

Industrial Revolution The social and economic shift that occurred in the mid-1700s from an agricultural society to a society that used machines to produce goods in factories

industry Business in which many people work and make money producing a product

International Space Station A very large building in space where astronauts from all over the world go to study space and science

landforms Natural features on Earth's surface that have distinct shapes, such as mountains

landmark A building, structure, or place that is worthy of notice

mass produce To make things in large amounts

microprocessor A part in a computer that controls what the computer does

multicultural Composed of groups of people from different backgrounds and heritages

neoclassical Referring to a return to ancient Greek and Roman styles of art and architecture

petroleum An oily liquid that is used to make gasoline and other products

phonograph A record player

plateaus Broad, flat lands that have higher elevations than plains

preserved To have kept something from being lost

producer A person or a group that makes something

regions Different parts of Earth that share a common characteristic, such as rainfall or a landform

service industries Businesses in which employees' job is to help or do things for other people, instead of producing goods

skyscrapers Very tall buildings

source The place from which something starts

tornadoes Violent funnel-shaped windstorms

tributaries Small rivers or streams that flow into larger rivers or streams

transcontinental railroad Train system that crossed the United States

urban Relating to a city

wetlands Land that is covered by water or that has a lot of moisture in the soil

 # Index